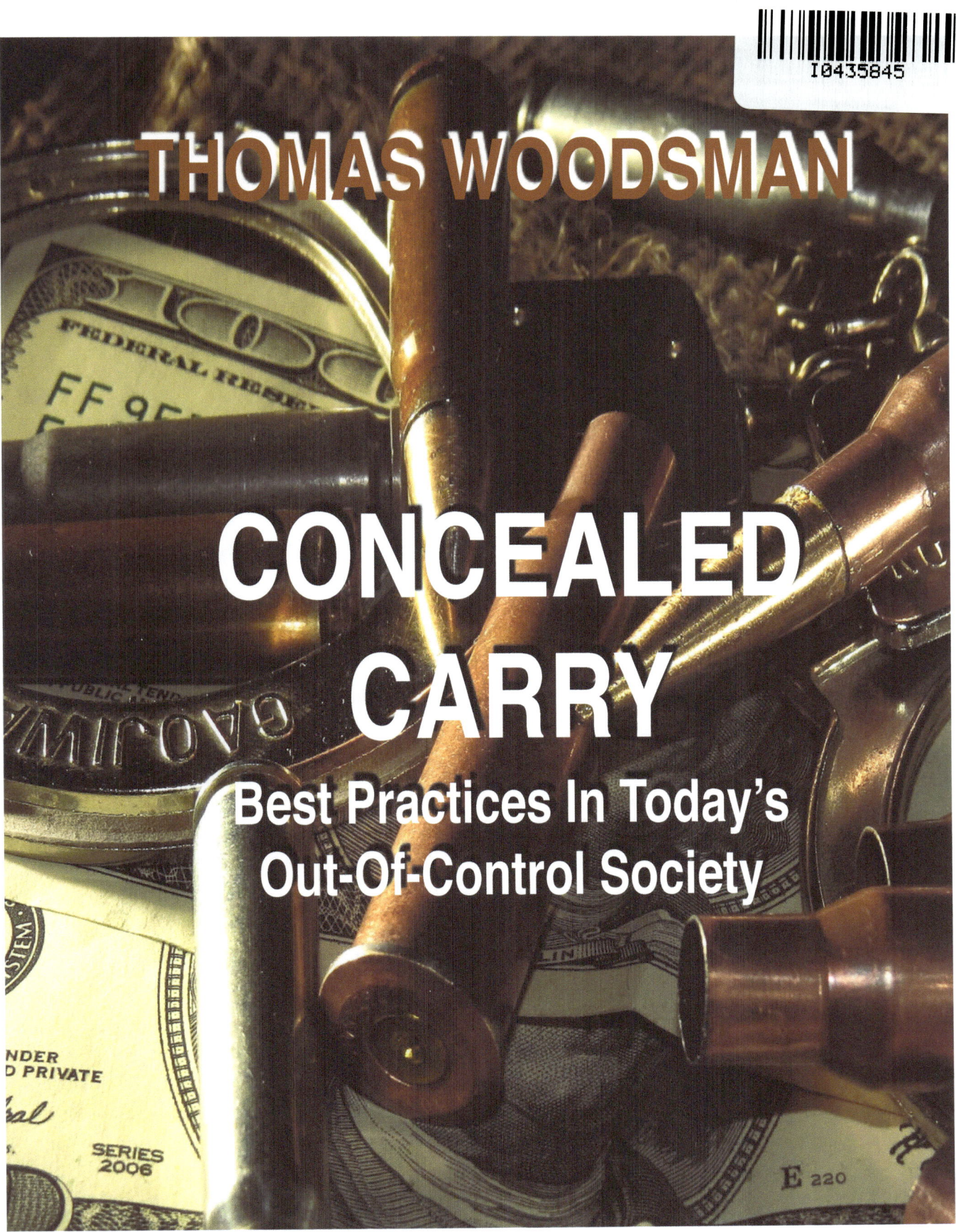

THOMAS WOODSMAN

CONCEALED
CARRY

Best Practices In Today's
Out-Of-Control Society

Carrying a Concealed Weapon

For many people, carrying a concealed weapon is one of their most important rights. Self-defense is crucial in many situations and being able to do so legally and effectively is very important. But there is some risk involved in carrying a weapon, no matter the legality of it. Being properly licensed and knowing the regulations that are associated with that license is an important responsibility of every person who carries a concealed weapon.

It is also crucial to know venues and locations in which it is always illegal to be carrying a gun. Each state has specific regulations concerning these locations, but all of them are intended to protect the best interests of every person. Two venues that guns are generally excluded from include most school campuses and large sporting events. In both of these situations, the misfire of a weapon or threatening brandishing of a weapon could cause a great deal of panic. To deal with this threat, carrying a handgun is completely illegal whether a person is properly licensed or not.

Many federal or governmental buildings also have restrictions concerning carrying weapons. Because of the sensitive nature of the operations of some of these buildings, safety is a primary concern. The safety of the people and information in these buildings is a high priority and generally important for public safety. These restrictions often include police stations and other public service stations as well. Carrying a gun on these premises can result in serious charges and consequences.

It is important for every person who carries a concealed weapon to be aware of the regulations of their state.

Easy Ways To Make Your Hands Stronger for Shooting Your Concealed Weapon

As anyone woman who has ever been shooting knows, a female's hands can get tired from all that trigger pulling and gun toting. Here are some easy ideas to strengthen your gun shooting hand without having to hit the gym to do it.

Gardening. Pulling weeds, digging and planting are all great exercises for strengthening the muscles in the hands and arms.

Snow shoveling. If you live in a seasonal weather state, shoveling snow and raking leaves are great opportunities to exercise your hands. Dress appropriately and wear gloves to avoid blisters or frostbite.

Crafts. By engaging in a variety of crafts, such as knitting, embroidery, or scrapbooking, you will flex the muscles in your hand, keeping them agile. Although making crafts might not strengthen your hands, it will make your hands more flexible.

Dry fire practice. The tried and true method to strengthen your hand and it won't cost you a bucket of money in ammo. Or, alternatively, try practicing with airsoft guns, a less expensive alternative to live ammo. Either way, using your hands will strengthen your muscles.

Practice your draw. If you've chosen to use a conceal carry purse to hide a weapon, regularly practice your quick draw, aim and shoot. You can also dry fire practice, saving the expense of ammo.

Dishwashing. No, don't wash them with a dishwasher. Wash your dishes the old fashioned way, in the kitchen sink. Not many of us do this anymore, but all the swishing and lifting are good movements for both hands and arms.

Lifting. If your kids are little (even if they don't feel so little), lifting and carrying them frequently will get your arms toned quickly. You'll be amazed how strong you become when you have children.

Swimming. If you have a pool or a nearby lake or water area, take some time to swim laps or engage in splash play. Water activities will strengthen your arm muscles and enable you to have a steady grip.

Flexilibity. Keep your hands nimble and your fingers flexible by playing cards, drawing with pencils or crayons, shooting rubber bands at targets or at the wall, braiding your hair or even sorting clothes and tieing socks together inside out. You want your fingers to be strong but also nimble.

By exercising your hands, fingers and arms on a daily basis, you will be fit and strong every time you ready your weapon for a day at the gun range.

How to Tell If Someone is Carrying a Concealed Weapon

When it comes to finding out if the individual that is threatening you has a weapon on him or not can be a difficult task for you don't want any surprises along the way if you have to get physical. Here are some ways you can spot or pick up signs that your enemy is carrying a concealed weapon in self defense situations.

-Wearing a concealment garment such as a jacket when it is noticeably too hot to be wearing clothing like that.

- Wearing a coat that is unzipped when weather is cold

- Wearing a shirt with the tail out and or only buttoned near the top. Note: Most thugs do not carry a gun in a holster. The most common method of carry is to slip the gun inside their waistband near the front pocket of their pants or in the small of their back.

- Repeatedly touching the area where you would likely carry a gun to adjust it when walking.

- Keeping one hand in the pocket to keep the gun stabilized or to camouflage the print of the gun through the clothing.

- When running, pressing a hand against clothing in an attempt to stabilize the gun.

- When your enemy is walking towards you he only swings one arm, using the other arm to stabilize the gun or to prevent concealment garment from opening.

- At the stand off, your enemy looks down *q*uickly to where the gun is concealed and moves his hand towards it.

- Look out for clothing that tugs more to one side because of the weight of the firearm pulling on it.

- The centerline of the pants in the crotch or buttock area pulled excessively to one side due to the gun being placed inside the waistband.

- Bulge under his clothes in the waist area.

- Bulky pockets.

- Imprint of the shape of the gun against the clothing or actually seeing the gun

- Hearing the sound of something solid (the gun) striking a door frame or counter when your enemy is walking towards you.

Remember "situational awareness" is one of your greatest weapons along with your mindset when it comes to your self defense and personal protection. for if you can see a threat coming, you can either avoid it or respond to it.

Best Concealed Carry Methods

So, just how do you hide your weapon?

Bear in mind: Allowing your weapon to be seen is called "brandishing", and depending on your area, is most likely prohibited. When you carry a concealed weapon, you have to make sure you take all safety measures so that you can easily conceal your weapon without risking it being seen.

There are several means to carry a concealed weapon. Exactly how you hide your weapon is up to you and will be based on a number of elements, such as clothing, environment, work circumstance, simplicity of access, etc.

Conventional Belt Holster

Conventional Belt Holsters are amongst the most extensively advised approaches of concealing your weapon.

Inside-the-pants holsters, external holsters, shoulder holsters and small of the back holsters are all suggested at different times.

Pros

    Easy
    Functional
    Easily concealed under a jacket or loose piece of clothing
    Ideal for a speedy draw

Cons

    Can not normally be used with a t-shirt or other tight fitting clothing since it will more easily print
    Easily exposed if coat or loose piece of clothes removed
    Can be uncomfortable when sitting

Fanny Pack

There are big and small fanny packs especially made to hold a concealed firearm. It is usual for concealed carry fanny packs to come with numerous areas for extra magazines, flashlights, etc

Pros

    Does not interfere in everyday tasks
    Completely independent of clothes (you do not need to use a coat or loose piece of clothing to conceal it)
    Easy to utilize and remember, as it is connected to your person
    Blend in with others who hold fanny packs for individual use

Cons

Does not go with formal dress (suit, dress, etc.)

People carrying concealed weapons, well-informed civilians, or police officers could recognize your concealed carry fanny pack for exactly what it is

Day Pack/Back Pack

If you prefer to carry and conceal a larger firearm, or simply want the extra storage space, a day pack or back pack is an additional option to carry your concealed weapon.

Pros

Extra storage space
Easy to hold
Very discreet

Cons

Poor access
Must take it off to sit down or do some tasks

Purse and Shoulder Bag/Briefcase

Women can easily carry concealed weapons in their purses, and everybody can easily conceal a weapon in a shoulder bag or briefcase. Specific concealed carry models are readily available.

Pros

Can be worn with formal dress (suit, dress, etc.)
Discreet
Extra storage

Cons

Target for thieves (purses especially)
Can be put down and forgotten

Thigh Holster (Women)

When using a dress or skirt, ladies may opt for a thigh holster.

Pros

   Very discreet
   Can be worn with formal dress

Cons

   Must be mindful of the height of your hem when sitting down so it does not ride up
   Take care when sitting to keep legs firmly together

Ankle Holster

For little concealed carry weapons, an ankle holster can easily be worn, particularly with boots.

Pros

   Very discreet with boots or loose pants
   Light and out of the way

Cons

   Awkward access
   Can not use with tight pants or short pants

Photographer's Vest

A really functional piece with lots of storage space, a photographer's vest can easily be used for concealed carry.

Pros

   Large, secure pockets
   Lots of storage space
   Lightweight

Cons

   Does not go with formal dress (suit, dress, etc.)
      People carrying concealed weapons, well-informed civilians, or policeman could recognize your concealed carry photographer's vest for just what it is

Holster Shirt

Holster your compact handgun in your shirt with a holster shirt.

Pros

   Lightweight
   Easy to wear
   Very discreet

Cons

   Poor availability (need to unbutton or open your top/outer shirt to access your firearm)

Pocket

If your firearm is little enough, you might be able to fit it inside of your pocket. It is much easier to fit inside of a jacket pocket, but you might additionally be able to use a cargo pant pocket or something comparable.

Pros

    Easily available
    Can be discreet

Cons

    If you are making use of a coat pocket, you might leave the coat behind
    Can just fit rather compact weapons in an ordinary pocket
    May be unbalanced unless you carry extra magazines in another pocket

Other/Unconventional

There are many other means to conceal your weapon, but you should keep in mind that the first goal is to keep your weapon out of sight and hidden. Below are some unusual concealed carry options, mainly for very little weapons.

    Change purse
    Specialty accessories (belt buckles, pocketbooks, holster grips)
    Belt pouch
    Hollowed out book
    Paper bag
    Cigarette case
    Camera case
    Package
    Bra

Is a Concealed Firearm Permit Enough?

Of all the reasons to carry a concealed weapon, the most compelling is self-defense. A recent Gallup poll reports 67% of American adult gun owners have their weapon "for protection against crime." If you are one of those who own or are considering purchasing a weapon for self-defense, the data would suggest that your logic is sound. One survey of male felons in 11 state prisons across the United States found that 40% of them did not commit a crime because they either knew or believed that the victim had a gun. In the same survey, 34% of the felons claimed to have been "scared off, shot at, wounded, or captured by an armed victim."

The Concealed Firearm Permit

The first step for most defense-motivated gun owners is a concealed firearm permit (CFP). The permits grant holders the right to carry a weapon (usually a handgun) in public in a concealed manner, such as under a jacket or in a purse. While the requirements and limitations on permits vary from state to state, CFPs have become popular nationwide. Utah, for example, has over half a million active permits in circulation, with 62% being held by non-residents. This popularity is due largely to the fact that any eligible person can obtain a Utah CFP in under five hours. The permit, which is recognized in 35 states, is a practical choice for most of the nation's gun owners.

Firearm Self Defense

Because of the relative ease of obtaining a CFP, many new permit holders may find themselves underprepared to effectively use their weapon in self-defense. If a gun owner is incapable of effectively wielding their weapon, it becomes a liability instead of an asset in a threatening situation. Because of this, it's a good idea for all gun owners to receive professional instruction. Training can make gun owners more safe and effective in a self-defense situation.

Basic firearms courses teach essential principles of responsible gun ownership and the basics of firearms. These courses focus on foundational gun use skills and teach students how to safely handle and store a firearm.

It is vital that all gun owners gain this fundamental knowledge so that they can safely pursue further training.

Once a student understands the basics of firearms, it seems obvious that they should become confident firing their handgun. Professional instruction can teach good technique and help a student avoid bad habits that are common to new shooters. It seems obvious that learning to hit your target should be a priority, but too many gun owners overlook this essential component to self-defense.

Defensive Pistol Course

Finally, a CFP holder with a good foundation should consider a defensive pistol course. These courses teach students to use their weapon in high-stress environments. Skills such as weak-hand shooting, shooting while moving, and combat-style reloading are covered. These courses are designed to help defense-minded gun owners learn to be as effective as possible when it counts the most.

If you've decided that gun ownership for your personal and family defense is something you'd like to pursue, obtain the training necessary to wield your weapon safely and with confidence. Seeking proper instruction will increase your odds in an emergency situation and give you the skills to fully enjoy shooting as a hobby. Remember: when it counts you could have just seconds to act. How well you've prepared could make that difference.

Dealing With Traffic Stops and Law Enforcement Officers While Carrying A Concealed Firearm

When being stopped by law enforcement for a traffic stop and you are carrying a firearm, it's always wise to stand in the officers shoes and view the situation from the officers perspective. The following steps on how to deal with law enforcement during a traffic stop isn't in the Florida 790 statutes, in fact the statute is pretty fuzzy on how an individual is expected to interact with law enforcement. Here's where we're going to apply a little common sense to make our lives easier.

When we see the flashing lights and hear the siren of a police car signaling us to pull over...

1. We should pull over as much as possible to the right of the roadway, giving the officer the courtesy of maintaining his/her personal safety. The officer getting out of his vehicle stands the possibility of being injured by passing vehicles, allow the officer as much space as possible, he will appreciate the fact you considered his personal safety.

2. Roll down all your windows, especially if they are tinted. If being stopped at night, turn on your interior light. This will allow the officer to clearly see in your vehicle. By doing this, you're in essence demonstrating to the officer that you're being polite, are ready to deal with him and have nothing to hide in your vehicle.

3. Turn off your vehicle and leave the keys on the dashboard. This will demonstrate to the officer you are not planning to flee the traffic stop.

4. Place your hands on the steering wheel at the 10 O'clock and 2 O'clock positions. This is a natural relaxed position that will demonstrate to the officer you're not going to try to reach for something that may injure or kill him.

5. When the officer walks up to your window, "if you have a concealed weapons permit", maintain both hands on the steering wheel and immediately inform the officer that you indeed have a concealed weapons permit and where your firearm is located on your person.

6. When the officer asks to see your, drivers license, insurance, registration and concealed weapons permit, have all the documents in one location, within easy reach and ready to hand the officer.

7. The officer may ask to inspect your firearm, he has every right to do so. Do not attempt to handle or reach for your firearm. Maintain both hands on the steering wheel and ask the officer how he/she would like to proceed and follow all orders.

Implementing the aforementioned 7 steps when being pulled over while carrying a firearm will calm the officers fear of the individual he just pulled over being a possible threat to his life.

This is something rarely discussed as part of a concealed weapons permit class but it's an important topic never the less. I hope this article enlightens everyone on how to better deal with traffic stops while carrying a concealed firearm.

Concealed Carry Clothing

When keeping your firearm concealed is your top priority, you'll need good clothing to do the job.

If you are carrying concealed and your clothes let you down by printing or causing you to brandish your weapon, you could be in a world of hurt and face major consequences.

Printing is caused by clothing that is too tightly pressed against your weapon and/or holster. The weapon then 'prints', or shows, through your garment. Clearly, this means that you are not carrying concealed.

Brandishing is when your weapon becomes visible. While carrying concealed, your gun has to be hidden, and if your shirt lifts up, or your jacket opens, revealing your gun, you can face charges.

Therefore, you must find clothing that is both loose enough to comfortably conceal your gun/holster without printing, and long/big/fitted enough to stop you from brandishing.

To carry concealed, you can do one of two things when it comes to clothing:

1. Wear Normal Clothing Effectively

2. Wear Specialized Conealed Carry Clothing

Wearing Normal Clothing Effectively

Your environment will dictate what kind of clothing you will wear.

Obviously, if you are performing manual labor, your outfit will be different than if you are a business executive.

However you dress, keep common sense in mind.

Concealed Carry Tops

Make sure that your shirt is either big enough and long enough to cover your firearm if you're carrying with a waistband holster. For casual wear, a long shirt (t-shirt, polo, button-up) will do, as long as it is not too tight and will not brandish if you sit down or the wind catches it.

If you tuck your shirt in, make sure you are wearing an appropriate holster (inside the waistband or non-waistband). While this limits your access, it is a very effective way to conceal your weapon.

Always make sure that concealment and accessibility are top of mind when it comes to shirts, but just make sure your clothing covers your gun.

Other tops, such as vests, sports jackets, blazers and coats are also good for concealing weapons.

Photographer's vests are commonly used to conceal firearms, because they are useful for storing other necessities, such as a flashlight and ammunition.

Blazers and sports coats are usually good, but make sure you keep them buttoned up to stop them from opening too widely, thereby revealing your weapon.

Similarly, jackets or coats are a great way to conceal your weapon, but make sure you only rely on a jacket for concealment if you are staying outside. You will raise questions if you are wearing your jacket inside all the time.

Concealed Carry Bottoms

Make sure your pants fit properly. Just like shirts, they can allow printing, and in some cases, brandishing.

If you carry inside the waistband, make sure the pants fit comfortably with your firearm.

A top priority is a good, sturdy belt to go with your pants, if you are using a waist holster. This will give you the rigidity and support you need for drawing your weapon quickly and efficiently.

Cargo pants work well, because you can either pocket carry, or at least utilize the cargo pockets to conceal ammunition or other add-ons.

Wear Specialized Conealed Carry Clothing

Concealed carry clothing is available from various manufacturers, and is made explicitly to conceal firearms on your person.

There are shirts, undershirts, belts, pants, jackets, purses, bras, and various other garments that are tailor-made to keep your gun hidden.

Unlike normal civilian clothing, concealed carry clothes are designed with concealment and accessibility in mind. There are shirts that have snap-away fronts and side vents for easy access, undershirts with pocket, and all sorts of other helpful products.

You must first know how you carry. If you are new to concealed carry, try out what works for you before thinking about concealed carry clothing. If you carry on the waist, take into consideration length of shirt, tightness of shirt/pants, etc. If you carry on the ankle, make sure you have low cut shoes and a wide legged slack.

To summarize, you can wear everyday clothes smartly, or you can get dedicated concealed carry clothing. Just make sure that you are going for concealment and accessibility. Comfort is also important, so that you do not give yourself away with uncomfortable fidgets and rearranging.

Five Reasons For Women To Own A Concealed Carry Purse

The headlines can be frightening. Break-ins, carjackings, robberies. Across the country, women are signing up for self-defense classes at record levels. Many women are considering the purchase of a gun for additional protection.

Women, in fact, are the fastest growing demographic of concealed carry permit holders. Women are also the fastest growing group of gun purchasers in the country. In nearly every state, courses that teach firearm safety are full and often have waiting lists.

If you are trying to decide whether or not to carry a concealed weapon, here are some reasons to consider:

* Carrying a weapon means that you can protect yourself and your family at all times

* Learning to use a gun is a useful life skill

* Self-protection is the responsibility of every woman, and a gun is a great step in taking charge of your own protection

* If the worst happens and you become the victim of a crime, you will likely be very glad you are carrying a gun

* A gun can also be used as a deterrent

If you decide that carrying a concealed weapon is the right decision for you, the first step is to check the CCW laws in your state. Some states have fairly easy regulations and some are very strict, making it difficult, if not impossible to obtain a permit. Be sure to get the required training.

Most CCW class instructors suggest that women do not purchase a weapon until after they have completed a training class. Instructors often believe that women benefit from trying different weapons during class and figuring out which guns they like to use the most. Some women prefer a small handgun and others like the feel and power of a large weapon.

The method of concealment needs to be considered. Holsters are the most popular carry method for men. A holster needs to be comfortable and needs to keep your weapon out of sight at all times.

However, even though women are the fastest growing market for purchases of weapons, few holsters are manufactured specifically for women. Asking other women which holsters they use can be helpful in finding a comfortable holster. Using the internet can also be a great resource.

The most popular method of concealment for women remains a purse. Here are five reasons why purse carry remains the concealment choice for most women:

Concealed carry purses contain special pockets, pouches or concealment areas designed specifically to hide and holster a gun.

Most CCW purse manufacturers build a holster right into the handbag.

A quality CCW purse allows easy grasp and draw of the weapon while providing a sturdy platform and hidden compartment.

Many purses also contain a lockable zipper, helping women keep guns away from their children.

Although carrying a concealed weapon is a big decision, it is every woman's job to take responsibility for her own safety. For many women, carrying a gun is the right choice to protect themselves and their families and a CCW purse helps them keep the gun within reach at all times.

Self-Defense Weapons - What Do They Say About You?

These days, there are more and more self-defense gadgets being invented, produced, and marketed than ever before. You can buy everything from cellphone tasers and electrified, no-touch jackets to knives hidden in lipstick tubes. What do these weapons in disguise say about you as a martial artist?

Useful Disguised Weapons

You probably don't want to read this, but the most useful disguised weapon is no disguise at all. The best weapon is an everyday object ... either something impromptu or a regular object, like a ball point pen, that you carry with you.

Of course, anything utilized as a weapon can be deemed a weapon in a court of law. But a disguised weapon has a hidden element. The courts will perceive it as a concealed weapon, almost every time.

Note: I am not a lawyer. So, I am not offering legal advice. The above is just a statement of observation. You need to take legal responsibility for your own actions.

Still, if you are determined to carry a disguised weapon, then make sure it's practical. If you can't use it in an emergency, then what's the use of having it?

Useless Secret Weapons

A concealed weapon becomes impractical if you can't get to it in time. A tube of lipstick in your purse won't help you in an attack, if ... it's in your purse.

You'd have to unsnap or unzip the purse, find the lipstick (oops, that one is a real lip gloss), get the cap off, and twist up the concealed blade ... all while you are being attacked.

Not likely.

If you have your weapon at the ready, then it is "less concealed." And you might be showing your attacker that you have something, if you aren't good at concealment.

And if your weapon is put away, then you have to be able to get to it and get it into play, all while adrenaline is coursing through your body. Have you ever tried precise, motor-skill actions while completely afraid?

It's next to impossible.

You need a basic weapon that you can get to.

Weapon Crutch

There are three types of people who buy disguised weapons. Your relationship to your weapon says a lot about you:

People with no martial training whatsoever buy a weapon as a substitute for skill. In their minds, sending 25,000 volts into someone trumps any martial-arts skill. (Not always the case, by the way.) Take away the weapon and they have nothing. No training to rely on. Game over.

The second type of customer is the martial artist -- one who lack confidence in his or her skill. Take away their weapons, and they panic. These are the types who rely on their weapons too much.

Finally, some competent martial artists buy a weapon to carry hidden. They know how to fight with or without the disguised (or concealed) weapon. The weapon only comes out in a self-defense situation, and often not too early in the confrontation....

Some of The Best Martial Artists Carry Weapons

This third group has a healthy understanding of weapon use in a fight. They don't want to face a judge having to explain what happened. On the other hand, the weapon is there ... just in case of an emergency.

If a fight seems overwhelming, out comes the weapon. And even here, it may be revealed as a surprise. No advanced warning.

Some of the most skilled martial artists out there carry concealed weapons. They don't rely on them, but they do carry them.

If a master martial artist loses a weapon during an altercation, it's not the end of the world. The weapon isn't a crutch. So, the master almost doesn't notice it's gone.

He or she fights equally well with or without a weapon. It's better not to "have to" rely on one.

One last thought ... what would you do, if your attacker got hold of your weapon, maybe a knife, and used it against you?

It's a real possibility. Are you prepared?

The Safe Route: Defensive Weapons In Your Car

You may have seen video on YouTube or on the evening news. Robbery or carjacking caught on video tape puts nausea in the pit of the stomach. There probably isn't any better reason why concealed carry gun laws are important. Additional defense weapons can be of value as well.

Things happen in a car that can lead to irreversible unhappiness. If tempers flare over poor driving, road rage can happen that gets someone killed. Road rage is most common on the fastest interstates in the country. Higher speeds lead to less room for errors and a mistake can set off unfortunate events.

For these reasons, your family benefits from defense weapons carried in the car. If you don't feel comfortable with a firearm, then a pepper spray canister is highly recommended. Pepper spray comes in different formulations these days.

There are stream and fogger pepper sprays. There are also the newer foams and gels. The foams and gels have the stickiness and viscosity to stick on an attackers face, causing a far more debilitating effect.

If you seek a larger range of safety then consider a pepper spray gun. A Mace gun is probably the most commonly purchased. This device has easy to use canisters that slide right into the rear of the gun's barrel. The canisters are contain one ounce of pepper spray. The beauty of the Mace gun is that a 25 foot stream of pepper spray is developed from the pressure in the gun, giving you ample distance from your attacker.

Add a simple pepper spray with a visor clip, for rapid deployment in surprise attacks. Surprise attacks happen. Most criminals know the element of surprise is one thing they have in their favor. Your advantage comes from carrying concealed weapons to end their crime rampage.

Automobile self defense includes other important tools as well. A diversion safe can be placed in the trunk to hold cash and valuables. The hidden can safe may be made from a can of engine degreaser or lubrication product or other ordinary automobile maintenance product. A thief is unlikely to check the can for a hidden compartment.

Or also consider what may happen if an accident causes some one to be trapped in their car. A cool tool to keep handy for roadside emergencies is the 4-n-1 Auto Emergency Tool. The tool consists of a seat belt knife, a window breaking tool, a standard flashlight and a magnetic blinking strobe light that is positioned on the car to alert other drivers.

Also consider at home installing a driveway sensor alarm. These devices detect the presence of movement in your driveway. Whether there is a stranger, a returning teenager or the family dog crawling under the car for shade, you will be alerted of any added dangers.

The tools discussed above can make a big difference in your driving safety. If you use and live near an interstate where the scofflaws laugh at the 65-70 mile an hour speed limits then you should take immediate steps to improve your driving self defense quotient. Your family deserves the protection.

How You Can Avoid a Carjacking Without Using Your Concealed Carry Weapon

Almost 50,000 attempted carjacking cases occur each year in the United States. Most do not succeed. However, some of them result in car theft, rapes, beatings or even murder.

If you're carrying a concealed gun in your handbag and someone attempts a carjacking, you might choose to use your weapon. However, before risking your life by possibly getting involved in a shooting, try to avoid your vehicle being carjacked in the first place.

Always park in well-lit areas

No matter where you go, make sure that your car is parked in a well-lit area. Carjackers will hesitate to act if they can be seen or heard by people.

Keep your strong hand free

While you are approaching your parked vehicle, keep your strong hand available, and the keys in the other. In case you are attacked, you will have time to land a surprise punch into your aggressor's face or a kick to the belly or crotch, and run away.

Attitude

Too many times, women are targeted by carjackers because they look like the perfect victims, meek and unable to fight back. While you walk towards your car, keep your head up and scan the area. Carjackers do not usually approach car owners that look guarded, and prefer victims that are more oblivious to their surroundings.

When you get in your car, put your bag on the floor

Carjackers are often tempted by a bag or a laptop left in the car. Consider hiding or keeping important items on the floor of the vehicle, so they cannot be easily spotted from the outside. Also, if you keep your gun in your bag, make sure to take it with you, even if you leave the vehicle for a short time. The last thing you want is to provide a potential attacker access to a weapon.

Lock your doors and drive away

Women are more likely to become victims of a carjacking because before starting a car they tend to spend time putting their things in order, putting on a seatbelt and so on. This gives any possible attacker the necessary time to act. As soon as you are in the vehicle, lock the doors and drive away. Put your seatbelt on once you get away from your parking area.

Avoid making physical contact with the attacker

In case of a carjacking, the most common sense advice is to leave the car and save your life. Try to throw your keys away from your attacker or toward the passenger area of the car, giving you time to get away. Making an attacker search for the keys can provide valuable time for an escape.

Be assertive

If you have your child in the car, do not waste any time. Just say 'my child is in the backseat', while you unbuckle the belt and take him or her away. Never wait for the carjacker to give you permission, just act fast and be determined. Grab your child and go.

Only half of all carjacking attempts succeed. Your gun should be a last resort. By staying informed, aware and vigilant, you and your family can be safe too.

Non Lethal Self Defense Weapons For Self Defense

You never know when you are going to need self defense and when non lethal self defense weapons such as stun guns and mace or pepper sprays are going to come in useful. You can be attacked at anytime for any reason: rape, theft, sheer badness, who knows, they all happen to men and women every day of every week.

Yes, men. I can hear you think there, but men get mugged - of course they do, and also get raped. That's a well known fact in this sick society so unless you want to travel with a concealed gun everywhere, you should carry some form of non lethal self defense weapon. These include pepper sprays, mace, tazers and stun guns. However, there are certain aspects of them that you should be aware of before purchasing them.

The problems with guns is that people buy them and when the time comes they are either afraid to use them because it could kill their assailant, or don't know how. Some have even been known to fire a gun and injured themselves with the recoil. You only need a slight hesitation to fire and your assailant will be upon you and if you have a gun he will have no mercy.

However, few will hesitate with a pepper spray or a stun gun, and both are very effective, which is why in some respects these are better for general self defense than a gun. Guns have to be concealed, so there is no deterrent through the attacker knowing you have one. That means that if you carry a gun you will have to be prepared to use it, which also means that you will have to be prepared to kill a human being. While that is not a problem to some, it is to most decent citizens, man or woman, and so you are better without it, and better to be armed with something you can use without hesitation.

Hesitation can cost you your life in certain situations, so go for a stun gun or a pepper spray. The spray is very effective only if the assailant is not wearing glasses, so the stun gun is likely to be your best first choice. Keep one in your purse and the other in a coat pocket. You will only have time to use the one, but if your purse is stolen the stun gun might be useful to hit the attacker as he or she tries to turn and run away with the purse.

Here are some tips on how to choose your non lethal self defense weapon, and how to use it for self defense. First, decide which you prefer - a spray or a tazer or stun gun. The latter is very effective if you can get the skin or through light clothing, and the former if the attacker is not wearing glasses.

Learn how to use it when you buy it: use a target at average height than practice at various distances until you understand the limitations of your choice of weapon. In self defense, you will have to discharge your stun gun or pepper spray at just the right distance for maximum effect. Any more and you might either miss, or your spray will be too spread out to be effective. Any less and your spray will have to be more accurate, and your stun gun might not be effective since you won't be able to aim it properly to avoid heavy clothing.

One the distance is second nature to you, practice at various heights, simulating attackers of different sizes. Practice until you are proficient and can pull out your weapon and use it any height and the correct distance without thought. You won't have time to think, and in a real situation will have to react automatically - that is the skill that practice gives you.

Once have decided on one product stay with it. Don't change because if you do you will have to go through all that practice one again. Not all stun guns and pepper sprays are the same, and if you change your brand the distance and spread might be different.

It is important that you can defend yourself in the street since the streets of most major cities are becoming dangerous, especially at night. However, the more people that fight back then the more the rapists and muggers will be discouraged and, who knows, the actions of people like you might just make our streets safer. Nobody is going to continue if they know that they are liable to face somebody with a stun gun or mace spray.

Non lethal self defense weapons for personal self defense are becoming more popular because they work, and not only that but they give those that use them successfully a feeling of satisfaction. They give the muggers a feeling of something else.

Concealed Carry Belts

Most people overlook this critical component of concealed carry.

A belt is just as important as your holster. For security, accessibility, comfort, and ease, you must get a good concealed carry belt.

What To Look For in a Concealed Carry Belt

You've probably spent a lot of time thinking about and researching your perfect gun and holster. Now it's time to think about your belt.

A concealed carry belt must be thick and it must be firm. It needs to be made of leather (or a very thick, heavy duty canvas for casual/tactical wear), and has to have been expertly crafted.

You will be looking at a belt that is about 1.25-1.75 inches wide and could be.25 inches thick. Overall, a very thick, heavy belt.

Make sure the buckle is not overlooked. It must be as high *q*uality as the rest of the belt to keep everything in place and not break.

The Purpose of a Concealed Carry Belt

First and foremost, a concealed carry belt is to keep your holster rigid.

When you need your firearm, you are going to go by instinct and draw. If your belt is not strong enough, your holster will pull and warp and come with the gun to some degree.

Even this one or two second slow-down caused by a 'floppy' holster can cost you your life in a situation where you need to draw your gun.

You want to be able to pull your gun up and out of the holster without much movement from the holster.

Secondly, your belt should keep the weight of your firearm, extra ammunition, and accessories distributed evenly.

Not only should you be thinking about utility, but also comfort.

It is vital that you consider comfort in all of your choices when it comes to CCW. If something is uncomfortable, you are a lot less likely to do it.

Furthermore, if you are struggling with discomfort, you might fidget, adjust your belt/pants, or even be distracted. All of these things can give you away and might even stop you from performing well when you need to use your weapon. If you're uncomfortable, you can't put your full attention to scanning your surroundings for threats.

Make sure that you choose a belt that you will actually wear. Don't pick a casual belt if you typically carry when you are wearing a suit. Don't pick a dress belt if you never wear a suit or dress clothes. Not only will you not like wearing it, but it could give you away.

This leads to a final point on remaining inconspicuous.

If your belt looks way too big and out of place, it is likely that a casual observer may notice it and realize that you are carrying concealed. When choosing a belt, make sure that you have the right balance of rigidity, comfort, and concealment.

Self-Defense - What You Should Know Before Buying Weapons For Self-Defense

If you are planning to buy self-defense products, and have no idea which one to choose, this article will definitely save you both - time and money! If you are looking for something that is easy to use and carry around, then consider buying a pepper spray.

Pepper spray

Pepper spray is one of the best choices as a self-defense option for women.

Advantages:

It can be easily concealed,
easy to use
highly effective
affordable
ideal for women that are not comfortable with a gun

There are different kinds of types. Basically, you should choose whether you want it small and discreet, like a pepper spray in the form of a pen, lipstick (woman love this one) or a cell-phone? Or do you feel more confident with a bigger spray with several shots? What range are you planning to shot? Some offer a range of 12 feet and others are only effective at a range of 4-5 feet. In a subway against a single attacker, for example, the latter would give you enough protection. If you want more protection on the streets against several attackers, go for a bigger spray with a wider range.

Disadvantages:

they are illegal in some states, so check your state regulations before buying

if attacker is on drugs, pepper spray will have little or no effect

if there is even a slight breeze toward your direction, you will get a "doze" as well

Taser - Taser C2

First of all, let me clear it up: there is a big difference between Taser and Stun Guns! Taser is one of the most powerful and effective non-lethal devices that you can find on the market. The main difference between these two is that stun guns require you to make direct contact with the target. Unlike tasers, stun guns use a low amerage and require a higher voltage. Tasers are designed to subdue an attacker with an electro-shock. Taser has proven itself very effective, and as far as I know there is only positive feedback for Taser C2.

The Top Five Reasons For Using a Self Defense Weapon

How much is your life worth? How much would you spend if you could protect your life and those of your family? Is there a monetary limit on the cost of a self defense weapon? Are there other considerations when it comes to defending your self and your family?

Unfortunately many people use the cost of a non lethal self defense weapon as the prime criteria for making a selection. Cost should be a consideration but certainly not the main or only one. Here are four others.

Now don't get me wrong please. If you don't have a self defense product like a stun gun or pepper spray you certainly can still defend your self and your family. And conversely just because you have one doesn't mean you are immune from danger. There are still plenty of variables. More on that some other time.

Here's the point. Most stun guns and pepper sprays are less than $75.00; the majority are less than $25.00. You can get a great stun gun and pepper spray for less than $75.00.

I always recommend to my customers to have both a pepper spray and stun gun with them at all times and to have them for home car and on your person. Having them is not enough. You need to know how to use them and practice using them too.

Four other considerations in getting self defense products are:

EASE OF USE.

All stun guns and pepper sprays are easy to use and carry.

SIZE.

Most stun guns and pepper sprays are small enough to carry in a purse or pocket. They are easy to conceal.

DISGUISABILITY.

Several stun guns and pepper sprays are disguised as other products giving you the tactical advantage of surprise.

POWER.

Not all stun guns and pepper sprays have the same capabilities. The more power or range the better.

So when it gets down to making a decision on something as important as defending your self and your family don't let cost be your only criteria. Other factors are important too. Consider all five and get several self defense products to have with you at all times.